Contraflower

Edited by Sarah Annetts & Peter Johnson

Scriberazone

SCRIBERAZONE

Published by Scriberazone
PO Box 3849, Sheffield S2 9AG, United Kingdom

http://www.scriberazone.co.uk

Selection, introduction, notes on editors and
acknowledgements copyright © Scriberazone, 2005

A CIP catalogue record for this title is available from the British Library

ISBN 0 9550326 0 1

Typeset in Humanist 521 font.

Printed and bound by Gutenberg Press Limited, Tarxien, Malta.

CONDITIONS OF SALE

All rights reserved. No part of this publication may be reproduced, stored in a retrieval system, or transmitted in any form or by any means, electronic, mechanical, photocopying, recording or otherwise, without the prior permission of the publisher

This book is sold subject to the condition that it shall not, by way of trade or otherwise, be lent, re-sold, hired out or otherwise circulated without the publisher's prior consent in any form of binding or cover other than that in which it is published and without a similar condition including this condition being imposed upon the subsequent purchaser.

Contents

Contents	iii
Introduction	vii
Section 1: BEHIND MY DESK	1
Monday Morning	3
Rodent Olympics	4
Nine To Five	5
I Tell Her How Much I Despise Work	6
Computer Solitaire	8
Trash Girl	9
Deepest Afternoon	10
Resistance Is Futile	11
Section 2: EVERYONE IS TRAVELLING	13
Afghan Market, Peshawar	15
Praha	16
In A Lonely Crowd - Near Nagoya Station	17
Not In Africa	18
Zao mi je	19
River	20
The Sadness Of Stations	21
Letters Home	22
Platform	23
No Point To Being A Slow Lemming	24
Baggage Claim	25
Section 3: A NIGHT LIKE THIS	27
Dinner With A Tyrant	29
The Girl In The Nightclub	30
Milk	32
Too Much	34
Singing At Stars	35
Waiting	36
A Charm Against Insomnia	37
Section 4: QUIET CONVERSATION	39
Edible Poems	41
To The Desperate And The Proud	42
Polemical/Poetical	43
Communication	44
Reaching Out	45
Section 5: THE WEIGHT OF LOVE	47
You	49
Silvered	50
The Furthest Edge	51
Heavenly Body	52
Synchronicity	53

Lucky For Some	54
A Surfer	55
Absence	56
Breaking Up	57
Red Gold And Green	58
November	59
The Touch	60
Loneliness	61
Ciao Bella	62
Section 6: THE TIME ALL THE TIME	**63**
Minding The Infant	65
Me	66
How To Build A Father	67
What I Would Tell You	68
It Goes On	70
Bloaks Of A Surtan Aje	71
A Lost Man	72
Level II	73
The Man Who Speaks Four Languages	74
Wings	75
(The Last Day of Being) Twenty-Six	76
Section 7: WHILE THE SUN DANCED	**77**
Feel The Sun	79
Leeds	80
Field	92
Open House	93
Infinite Blue Sky	94
Party	96
Deux Mille Trois	97
Bubbles	98
Section 8: HE THOUGHT IT WAS REAL	**99**
Every Other Me	101
Our Last Supper Together in a Cemetery	102
Kicking Small Dogs	103
It's About Time	104
Zebra	105
Questions About Loss	106
Leaking Kerosene	107
Eyes In Midnight Skies	108
The Poets	**111**
The Editors	**113**

"That which sings and contemplates in you
is still dwelling within the bounds of that first moment
which scattered the stars into space"

- Kahlil Gibran

Introduction

I'm sure that like me you sometimes wonder: "where have all the rebels gone?" Is there still any kind of underground that hasn't been exploited by corporates and fashionistas for the sake of profit and kudos? The fact that you have this book in your hands means that you have stumbled upon what we consider to be a thriving alternative movement. We poets are considered so achingly uncool and incapable of making a respectable profit (in an age when cool and profit are kings) that the only place for our art is underground.

Poetry doesn't really sell – I am reliably informed that in the UK, the number of practitioners who earn their living solely from their art is less than ten! Poetry is definitely not cool – it's still pretty much seen as archaic, outmoded, and to be frank, weird. Radio 4's wonderfully 1950s *Poetry Please* is an example of where this art form sits in the public conciousness. Even the hip young experimenters who use poetry to embellish their musical creations (listen to Ty's *Music To Fly To* or Nathan Haines' *Springtime Rain*) refer to this as "spoken word". I'm not sure that they can bring themselves to utter the word "poetry".

So we're reduced to holding sparsely-attended events in smoky basements where writers and those few who appreciate our art assemble to create a vibe of beauty and honesty. Allow me a flight of fancy here: it feels sometimes that we are outlaws of emotion and truth in a world where materialism and mendacity rule with an iron grip. And like all conspirators throughout history, we gather in dark rooms with others of the same mind. The silver lining of this state of affairs is that – like the black-rimmed NHS-style spectacles of old – the decidedly uncool has a way of becoming the markedly hip.

In recent years the poetry underground has found the perfect medium in the internet. Here we have a potential audience of billions, low costs and a grapevine through which to communicate. *Scriberazone*.co.uk (pronounced Scribe-ra-zone) was born during the late 1990s dotcom boom and has published many talented poets whose work would not otherwise have seen the light of day. It also became very clear that individuals from all walks of life are writing poems and sending their work off to literary websites. This leads us to believe that the love of poetry may only be sleeping, not dead.

The contemporary nature of the work that is being posted on the internet affords us an opportunity to ask the public to take another look at poetry. This is a public who consume many forms of inspirational art: contemporary music, the visual genres, and the novel. They appreciate the beauty and depth of such creativity, as well as the inspiration it can engender.

However somewhere along the line many of these same individuals seem to have missed or misunderstood the fact that poetry can produce the same uplift as their other favourite works of art.

Of course, you the reader do need to put in a little effort to discover the magic within: you can't skim read poems! Nor should you try to read the entire book at one sitting. One of the great things is that you can dip in and out and choose to read pieces according to where your head is at - whether commuting to a boring job, in between bands at a summer music festival or in the park on a sunny Sunday afternoon.

So are you ready to try this? To dip your toe into something that you think you might not like? You may be challenged or repulsed; in fact all your prejudices may well be confirmed. But aren't undergrounds always this way? How many were initially repelled by the punks of '77 only to later understand the enormity of the paradigm shift that they represented? Recall the host of commentators who found hip-hop too harsh and lacking in soul. Those same voices now appreciate the manner in which Run DMC, Public Enemy and De La Soul changed our musical landscape forever.

Those of us who have discovered the corporate-free beauty and soul within this esoteric world of poetry know that if you read these pages with an open mind, your effort will be rewarded. But be warned: admitting to liking poetry sets one apart and demonstrates to others that you go against the flow. The payback is that within this underground, or should we say; this *contraflow*, you will find a new *flowering* of inspiration.

Peter Johnson
Sheffield
July 2005

Editors' Note:

Scriberazone's writers hail from half a dozen countries so there is no "standard" form of English which dominates. As a result, both US and UK spellings are used in this collection.

1: BEHIND MY DESK

Monday Morning

Morning! Monday Morning,
desperation leaks through my pores
as I open the office door
into a new week

Same carpets, same chairs
Same people same stares

I punch in my password
with such onomastic passion
that crumbs crunch under
my keyboard!

Shouting small talk across the room
"Nice weekend?"
"Gooooooooood!"
Don't spoil the memories
by sharing them with Jeffrey,
who still flies model aeroplanes,
at forty-three (wife and two kids)

Savour it,
dip your finger in
let the tips of your mind
be gently caressed
by moist reminiscence

Diarrhoeic emails, Staff meetings
kissed cappuccino cups
news on pin-stripe piss-ups,
welcome to the working week!

Rodent Olympics

I'm not sure that I'm very good
At racing these other rats
Most of them are so much faster
Than me.
I spend too much of my time
Dreaming that I'm an elegant
Swan,
To train (like the rest of them) at
Becoming proficient at the
2000cm sewer dash.
Perhaps I'll leave them to
Their sprinting
And go and watch the sea.

Nine To Five

As I set behind my desk
sinking into oblivion
I pray I will rise again
in some other world
to the sound of unicorns
chasing pipe dreams

I Tell Her How Much I Despise Work

and I prove it -

s t r e t c h ing my savings
over the blessed

time
of non-work

and

as the green dips
in the low,

my girlfriend's mood
follows -

knowing
that I either
get another job
or else

endure the wrath of words
handed to me by her

and her female
work companions -

offering the only advice
that they would offer
to those so different from
themselves.

but I ring her
after an interview,
with some luck -

there's a
teaching job
relieving the full-timers
when they fall sick

& immediately

she asks how much
my prospective weekly earnings

and I tell her
and coo-baby's the answer

& somehow
Brad's status soars sky-high
with a happy-o

and now all I have to do
is somehow hold
the job

as I tell her
how much I
despise work.

Computer Solitaire

I

You never really know what you did wrong.
It's not like in the old days when you could
lift a corner of the card you'd rejected
to discover what your future would have been like
in this game. It's never explained if
you've been lax, or silly or just dealt a bad hand.
The authority is blind, but I return to it every chance
I get, trying hard not to look
like the addict I am.

II

If in a busy office you catch
a clerk off balance,
or from behind, the chances
are he's playing a computer game,
looking very devoted and efficient
from without
but inside crying obsessively
for even a limited measure
of success in the world that counts.

Trash Girl

I am the lowly trash girl,
I haul trash
up and down a hill.
for red manicured nails
who think it is too menial

My reward?
A smug and smoggy sandwich
thrown away in the trash
by a high maintenance suburban poodle
who can't spell
gratitude.

I am grateful,
I humbly accept her trash
because it is my treasure.

Urban outfitter woman tries to starve herself to look beautiful,
ugly trash girl tries to feed herself to stay alive.
Urban outfitter woman places little value on food,
trash girl would give anything to have it.

Deepest Afternoon

Attempting to cut through
The thick, stifling jungle
Of deepest afternoon.

I am dulled, tired, slow
While outside a burning sun
And blanketing humidity
Reduces the pace of everything alive
Out there.

Some can only lie;
Lunch breaks spent succumbing
To the oppression
Staring upwards into space.
Others, like me
Vainly try to fight it,
Swinging the scythe of my
Intellect at the hazy heat.

The scythe is too blunt
Not even an ephemeral northern breeze
Can restore its edge
The words on the page that
I read become a lullaby
Sending me gently off to sleep

Resistance Is Futile

Every boss keeps telling me
That
Resistance is futile;

Even as I work with my union rep
Carefully
Chipping away their concrete blocks of workplace oppression

Every boss keeps telling me
That
Resistance is futile;

Fighting to get a work colleague
Off
A disciplinary

Or informing another that his lateness should
NOT
Impact on a limited pay increase opportunity

Every boss keeps telling me
That
Resistance is futile;

Just as my colleagues threaten a
Walkout
Due to the understaffing situation

And the process of staff unionization
Increases
Slowly but surely…

Your resistance,
Boss,

Is
Futile!

2: EVERYONE IS TRAVELLING

Afghan Market, Peshawar

Cutting a pale path
through the forest of brown eyes
I run to avoid the sudden storm

My shelter is a four storey caravanserai
with rickety stairs. It smells of rain on rubbish
of something sweet and rotting

The gold-sellers in the alleys outside
are sleek, trading in guns and opium,
Allah and America

but here are a million
shabby households, piled high
and going cheap

A nation has died and the relatives
resigned from grief
stack the debris of particular, peculiar lives

Lying on piles of dusty carpets
they proffer me sad smiles and Russian teapots
lapis on dulled silver

Iftah bread and prayers
rude winks, and all the paraphernalia
of Silk Route-treading horses -

things that once
were somebody's things
from places where people once lived

In the rainy dusk
deep in the dirty inner city,
I buy blue glass that shines like a tropical sea

and feel only the pity,
the pity.

Praha

Praha
Sun
Light on gilt

Water fountains down from golden gutters
Across sharp shadows,
Licks and cradles a pathway
Over small stones
    my bright boy stands there, frozen

Kafka frowns, because
    art flies around truth.

That's his perception, mind
And mine?
Truth wouldn't know itself round here, most times.

All I know, is
I'd walk across broken prisms
To fill the void between us

Praha
Heavy on guilt.

In A Lonely Crowd - Near Nagoya Station

The street before me stretches beyond sight,
I don't know where it ends,
maybe in hell or Tokyo

It's filled with teeming multitudes,
shoppers and punks and glamorous nobodies
in mismatched clothing for style less effect

They all want to be unique,
so make themselves identical,
and turn to rebellion through volume alone

Everyone is travelling in packs-
packs of grannies,
packs of wannabe pop stars and wannabe supermodels,

Packs of suited salary men,
united by their vomit stained shirt fronts-
no one is alone

It seems like they are all marching in circles,
nowhere to go, but going
home would mean solitude

Out here there is motion,
there is refulgence and chaos
and no thought of the bare box room
on the 28th floor

Not In Africa

I have never travelled through Africa,
and watched the sun set
on the Serengeti plains.

I have never crouched,
silent as the grave,
while a lioness tore apart a jackal,
or a bandy legged giraffe drank:
strange and beautiful.

I have never escaped
from a charging rhinoceros
with only a few scuff marks:
dusted myself down
and drank down the adventure
at a campfire dusk.

But once, in a safari park,
I locked the car keys in the boot
and watched my father,
surrounded by terror and monkeys
pick the lock with a fishknife,
wearing the calm look of someone
who has stared into the eyes of danger
and made danger back down.

Zao mi je (I'm Sorry)

Grey buildings
Blend into grey skies
Red sprayed on hatred
Adorns the walls
Bright boys swagger
With eyes black and dead
Dreams a thousand miles away
People they hate living them out
Shops sell foreign sweets
Children push cold noses
And empty bellies
Against freezing glass windows
Of fluorescent hope
And I walk by
My pockets full of money
My mouth an O of shame
Arms aching to hold their small bodies
And whisper lullabies of hope
Old men
Gather on corners
And reminisce
Leaning on sticks
The weight of their despair
Has broken their backs

River

Moving down a river, on banks, warehouses,
The nearest has had for years molasses
Spilled on its long loading platform.
As a child, I put my hands on its boards,
My hands arose sweet and gold.
Now in distance warehouses become
Haphazard smears and lines, as in a Franz Kline.
On black mud jetting out into rainbow hued water,
Reeds with criss-crossed green blades.
A night heron stands, humped in mystery,
The breeze lifts a white feather from its gray neck.
The only sounds of which I am aware,
Is the buzz of an insect I do not know,
One note repeated over and over by a warbler.
And the splash of my oars.
An otter sinks underwater, reappears in offshore stream.
White ibis send white reflections over oozing black mud.

I have no destination, but for once in my life,
I feel that I'm going somewhere.

The Sadness Of Stations

It is the goodbyes that linger,
more than the brief flames of welcome
that flicker, and then are gone.
Sorrows of parting take flight;
scatter the pigeons among the rafters
and sit, breathing the life from the air;
the sadness aching your chest.
Faces at the window
bear the tracks of their grief too clearly,
mirrored in the faces they roll away from
waving their slow farewell; as
under the eaves, the wings of their goodbyes
snuff out candles, one by one.

Letters Home

(1) Things I don't miss

I don't miss reading Bridget Jones
or the Daily Mail.
I don't miss lame excuses
from the former British Rail.

I don't miss hedges
and I never was too keen
on scotch eggs, Michael Barrymore,
Songs of Praise, the Queen.

I neither miss the Northern Line,
nor the Bakerloo.
I don't miss Carol Smillie.
I don't miss you.

(2) Things I miss

I miss the early-rising sky
which only shuts its bloodshot eye
after nineteen hours alert, unblinking.

I miss badgers, dormice, moles
and other shylife.

I miss fog that's yoghurt-white,
breath like ghostly bubblegum.

I miss the non-abusive sun
which fondles without bruising.

I miss dew.

Platform

she drops her bags
and walks into his arms

and i remember that feeling
like relief
and there is nothing round you
not the teeming platform
or the whine of the tannoy

not the escalators
bearing lines of people
upward to the light

there is only mouth on mouth
the hunger of eyes

i see
his hands in her hair
and something matters suddenly

i remember longing
how it's seated belly deep
a space where something ought to be
and how it makes you careless

i walk past them

lifted from the ordinary
they glow like saints

No Point To Being A Slow Lemming

At the end of a gaze, the window is an anchor
It's a time for goodbye, and a time to think
And drink in the green almost negligent vista
on the edge of another still and heavy day
This is what the mind will magnify later, the
colors and the somnolent hush of reds and browns
that underscore the absence of breeze at dusk
as the wind stops to catch its breath, tired from
all the ceaseless bustling amongst mangroves
and coconut trees and palm fronds and banyans
from all that rustling and melded fronds creating a
kaleidoscope painted with the colors it finds around
the green and yellow of papayas and cashews, red
blossoms of bougainvillea and the dark bottle green
of thottavadi povu, green patches of grass mottled
with the browns and blacks of mynahs and crows
all hung over with the golden purple majesty of
the inevitable sunset

And the dusk, gathering all available light
into that one ripe avalanche of glinting flight
that races into memory to unlock all that has
come and gone, to reweave the day into another
tapestry of color and smells, chembarathis and
mullapoovu and the erinjipoovu on ambalakaavus
building to a heady heady fragrance fused into
a redolent identity that cannot be separated
from this land, that we lay claim to in our mind

What if we could go back? - if we could go back into
the drenched monsoons, the sunscorched summers,
into the lazy drift and thrumming of backwater rivers,
sweeping around red-shawled hills along green-fringed
rivers ...all those various greens shading into soft blue
in the sudden falling of a sultry evening in the tropics

If the rippling waters spinning, spinning through us
could carry us back, taking us to what we know now
that we had to leave then. That we can't do that now
if we stop paying the price for the next round of progress
where would that leave us stranded in our lives tomorrow?

Baggage Claim

At the airport's large-intestinal tract,
we wait for what we packed yesterday,
conveyer belt contestants from The Generation Game.

Your case emerges first,
slender and stately.
Twenty-eight hours
and not a zip out of place.

My backpack burps and sprawls against a sports bag,
engorged and bored with lack of space.

Never one to drag its wheels,
your suitcase states there's Nothing to Declare.

My backpack waits, knows different.
Its guts are stuffed to bursting and it shows.

Your killjoy case struts off outside.
The carousel lays claim to mine.
I let it spin -
again.

3: A NIGHT LIKE THIS

Dinner With A Tyrant

She enters
his brittle queen
a brandy snap of
forced cream
and takes her throne
declaring dinner open

She sits
from head to toe
commanding attention
razor cropped haircut
complementing short tongue
steel tipped stilettos
nailing down insurrection

knowing his station
he sits
and emits
saccharine noises
we watch him
mould and fold himself
around her
like thick golden syrup
theirs is a refined love
so crystal clear

we, in attendance,
plod stately through
our train of courses
unable to eat dessert
I ask for gorgonzola
My sweet tooth is cured
I declare
Victoria is not amused

The Girl In The Nightclub

my back
found a column to rest my body,

and my eyes
found a wall to stare at,
to just stare at,

and I was beginning to
settle in nicely

when this woman
found my eyes

and began to dance
from side to side

her arms snaking
her hips and belly

showing...

parading their glorious whiteness

and my eyes
struggled with their fixation on the wall

but they held true,
they held faithful

in the only way a dog
could hold faith

and in a short while,
the dancer grew impatient, erratic,

her steps were showing
some frustration

as I smiled

and I began to discover
features on the wall,

there was smoothness and whiteness,
there were patient features.

features that I'd never seen before
and that one would rarely see on a woman

and the dancing girl began to struggle
and in between the songs - ice cubes,

out of her drink,
came my way.

but my eyes held true
to their need of this wall

and there may have even been
strong signals of courtship

but one never can tell
with courtship

their signals
can be so unreliable sometimes.

Milk

God bless the all night garage,
A gaudy strip-lit paradise.
The only movement
In a sleeping world.

Through petrol-stained puddles,
And fuel drenched air
I queue with the rest
To make my simple request.

Behind the lycra-clad ladies.
Who never go to bed
With the same man twice.
I ponder shrink-wrapped sandwiches.

Alongside the pothead
Candy seekers.
With faces pressed on glass,
like Christmas children.

Nervous shuffles in the queue,
As police slide by.
In short arsed hatchback
Panda cars.

I've done nothing.
But will I be
Guilty by association?
I only want a carton.

Something for my tea,
Something to help me sleep.
Am I the only one here
Standing up straight?

The car moves on
And the line relaxes.
The ladies clutch their coffee.
And advertise,
Burnt out wares.

I smile politely,
Decline their offers.

I'm not looking,
Not even browsing.

Pothead steps up,
To the window.
Fumbles his change,
And forgets why he came.

He points to the Pringles,
With saucerlike eyes.
He eyes up the chocolate,
And coins fall like rain.

He stoops to conquer,
His fallen handful
Of mixed bag copper,
And I take his place.

At the window,
I ask for milk.
Semi-skimmed,
Just a pint.

Oh… and a kit-kat.

Too Much

Awake
Grinding teeth
A mill from self.
I close my eyes but my eyeballs still dance,
Rushing around beneath that layer
Left right up down keep moving don't stop
What's happening, where, quick we want to know!
Black eyes
Giant pupils that take away the bright blue and replace it with darkness.
Do you remember the music?
You can hear it can't you?
There it is...
The drumbeat starts against the side of your head
Don't think about it, it will only get louder
Hear it more, and the pupils begin moving to the beats.
Left right up down
Where are the lights?
Nope
No light because we aren't there anymore.
I am lying on a bed with grinding teeth.
Teeth that are used to make our own music.
Can you hear it,
It goes with the rhythm of the side of my head.
No, the sun begins to rise and I am still here.
Still awake.
It might stop soon.
Let me out.

Singing At Stars

Not done. Not with full voice on clear frosty
nights
nor with a pose suggesting benediction and
blessing.
No, not done, but approved of and responded to
When
found in a poem where such things were done
and done
to good intent. And at once it's familiar.
As if
this was an art long practised and indulged in.
As if
singing with the voice alert to all the nuances
of light
was some nightly ritual by one who does not believe
in rituals.
As if the stars required it. As if by being
such singing
was necessary to affirm something permanent in
the flow
of time the stars observed. So I will sing now
not hum
but sing as passionate as one is when in love. I'll go
out
to the yard, assume a stance, and when the stars appear
sing
as if song were sufficient praise for their being.
Not done,
no, not yet, but already the act is familiar to me
who
has been a believer without the accurate means of praise
but who
now finds this to be an obvious act. Praise that it is!
Praise
that it should be so! Praise for such glory on a night
like this
when one wakes to the mode appropriate to stars
and standing
there in a jubilant pose sings and sings and sings!

Waiting

I watched the night sky
not for a star to follow
but for one that would fall
to the earth and show me
where to stand.

A Charm Against Insomnia

Moon, soothe this night
that thunders like horses
leaping cross the bed
then spinning to trot, gallop and leap
again and again, stirring the air
with old sorrows and dusty fears
Moon, let your fingers caress
the soft neck of sorrow, clearing
the fuddled passages, searing away
painful scars from tiny nerves.
Moon, you know the woe of sleeplessness,
have watched life reviewed and suffered in the night,
fathom the depths of cure.
Give of your wisdom,
your comfort:
Soothe this night.

4: QUIET CONVERSATION

Edible Poems

If I could only cook like that
So that you know

even while you are

eating - what

Beauty
has become
a part
of you

To The Desperate And The Proud

we
clamour for it

when we
need it the most.

Often,

it is when alone
that it hits

terribly...

like toothache,
like gout,
like the succeeding pangs
of diverse hungers.

our needs are not that varied:
some quiet conversation
in a dark room

with somebody

other
than ourselves.

Polemical/Poetical

POETS!

don't prostitute the art !

only speak with the voice
of your honest,
your open,
your longing or broken,

your shattered,
your scarred, marred,
bloody and battered,

perhaps quite outspoken
- yet fiendishly fragile and easily broken -

oh, only speak with the voice
of your honest, your open
HEART!

Communication

I lingered in the shadows waiting to be born,
my father was electricity and my mother was a human voice.

I woke the silence between continents with a burst of static
and a talent for mimicry that mankind had never known.

I was the standard bearer of sounds so familiar,
carrying them to all the places they had been but in ways they had never travelled.

I was stretched across time,
learning my craft and learning it well.
I crawled and then I walked and now I sprint wherever I go.
I launch myself ad infinitum and whiplash back and forth beneath the ocean.

First borne aloft on roads of copper and now highways of glass.
I scream across the air at the speed of imagination,
gathering pace with every passing second
waiting for intellect and innovation to guide me faster and faster.

I was anchored, tethered and tied to the Earth
yet now I leap into the sky like a bolt from the blue and out into the black.
I'm all around you on the ground and in the stars.
I carry your thoughts and your words and I convey your sadness and joy.
I bear tidings good and ill.
I can save lives, and sometimes end them.

I am an order for pens and paper,
I am a mother's good night kiss.
I'm the latest headline in the paper and a faded photograph remade anew.
I'm your blessing and your curse.

Now more than ever I follow you wherever you go,
I'll bounce off tin cans in the sky to be with you.
I'll take your precious, private moments and crumble them to dust.

I'm half a world away and I'm in the next street.
I am the bearer of all tidings.

Welcome to the Information Age.

Reaching Out

*"The poet is the specialist of emotion...I think it is the
duty of the poet to obtain citizenship for an increasing horde of Nameless
emotions..."*
- Agnes Nemes Nagy

I'm aiming at brutality, because the truth is brutal,
Learning things about yourself you never knew;
I'm aiming at that tenderness you never quite believed in
Till the day you found it welling out of you.

I'm speaking of the feeling when you catch upon her face
A look you never dared to hope you'd find;
I'm speaking of the sight of him with clenched and trembling hands,
When suddenly his sorrow floods your mind.

It's touching on that moment when your heart finds wings anew,
And you're aching with a joy beyond belief;
It's touching on the other, on the words you dare not speak:
Your shibboleth, your dark and nameless grief.

5: THE WEIGHT OF LOVE

You

I love the beauty of your deep thoughts
Those worries that knot and intertwine
Irrational and useless
The cause of delicate furrows on your brow

I love the beauty of your confusion
The simplicity of your questions
Endless questions
Like you only ever see the world for the first time

I love the beauty of your gestures
Those funny faces you pull
Even out of distaste
Those playful reactions or frustrations towards my words

I love the beauty that can be found beyond your eyes
When you smile or cry
That sensitivity that makes your sun shine differently
Strangely, as if you already have the answers

I love the beauty of your temper
Filled with a fire that cannot be put out
Because even when those flames burn
I know they cannot hurt me

Silvered

if a person
was made of mercury
and mercury wasn't cold,
but glowed
then that is me now,
lying here
asking
"where do you feel it?"

and if a person
could be lead
but lead was warm
and made its own light
i am that now
unable to lift a hand
for all the weight of love

i can't rise and when i can
will walk like a drunk, swim
along the wall, laughing

there is nothing better, i tell you
being silvered as a fish
"i'm luminous," i say

The Furthest Edge

now our road
runs apart
round winter's fields
on the furthest edge
of goodbye
write to me sometimes
in joined up writing
and warm me
with words
from your place of surprise

you come to me
i come to meet
we walk away
on the furthest edge
of goodbye
we turn and return
in continuous replay
as players
recalled
in whispering firelight

Heavenly Body

You -
Sleeping on your stomach
I -
See five perfect moles
Coiled around
The centre of your

S
 P
   I
  N
 E

A constellation lies
On
A heavenly body

Synchronicity

Incredible moment:
a heart and a heart
barely inches apart
meeting each other
beating as lovers
Indelible moment:
beautiful

omen

Lucky For Some

*"Every man I have loved
was like an army"*
- All Clear, Marge Piercy.

The men I've loved have been:
chick peas,
cotton buds,
worry beads,
the dormouse in *Alice*,
jelly beans.

I've paddled in puddles
when I want a tidal wave,
got guppies blowing bubbles in the dark.

I'm sick of crickets
so easily flicked away.

Give me a grunting,
growling
Maori warrior.

Give me a shark.

A Surfer

Do you know what makes you?
Tick.
Time gets impatient.

I leave you naked and alone
To surf through the surfer's bookshelf.
An unfascinating array
Of comic heroes, beer heroes,
Clinical heroes and sporting heroes.

Tick.
Waste of time.

Why do you surf only on the surface?
You skim on shaky, unsteady legs.
Do you ever want to let go
And dive deep into the crest of a wave?
Let go
And let exploding passion
Carry you wherever.

I caress your chiselled face.
I feel nothing from your hollow mask.

Tick.
Time pries open your eyes
Violently.

What are you?
What makes you?

Quick!
Let yourself fall.

Absence

Simply the silence in the absence of your voice is deadening;
I feel my fingers go cold - is that the cold?
Or missing you?

Breaking Up

And I drop it
and smash it
but it was chipped anyway
and you say
that's it
I'm gone
and I say
your porcelain heart
was useless
at least now
I can mosaic the bathroom

Red Gold and Green

This is it then
Today is the final
Goodbye
L'été deux mille trois
Has her hat and coat
The taxi's engine
Hums impatiently outside
She's now ready to
Go on her way.

And special as she is
Her goodbye is not
A simple, dreary affair;
She has conjured up
A Jackson Pollock
Landscape to remember
Her by
Reds and golds
And greens
Incandescent
In the fragile
Autumn sunshine.

We made love as the
Sun set today
Giving my love
To honour your love
Adieu

November

A time of mists and berries, yes –
But keep your 'mellow fruitfulness'.
This is the harder end of autumn; these
The days when warm September breeze
Is turned to bitter chill. It frosts the heart -
Appropriate, then, that we're apart
Now; the days long past
When it seemed that summer would always last
For us. I loved you then beyond all reason!
But this, my friend, -
This is the harder end.
This is another season.

The Touch

the touch of my lover
shakes the rattle in my soul
we roll with each other
he rocks me to and fro
he licks me like the cream
at the bottom
of his bowl

the touch of my lover
draws the water from my well
we roll with each other
he rings me like a bell
he feeds me the oyster
that is waiting
in the shell

the touch of my lover
teases joy that makes me cry
we roll with each other
he rides me to the sky
he squeezes very close
then he shows me
i can fly

Loneliness

a drizzle
is upon me
while she's gone away
tickling my thoughts
with whispered promises;
insulation from the lightning
of her fiery embrace

Ciao Bella

Sitting here,
Feeling like a beef dish
In a Creutzfeldt Jakob Disease clinic
Canteen.

I thought that we'd last forever
But we never did.
I watch the processes of dislike
Bubble up in your throat
Like bile
As you ready yourself to regurgitate
The past year's love all over me.

And am I sad?
You could cut out my heart with a small
Serrated sword
And the pain would be much the same.

I didn't realise how much I loved you
Until now,
When you've gone
And I stand here contemplating my navel
In the rain.

Ciao bella
You'll never be mia dolce again.

6: THE TIME ALL THE TIME

Minding The Infant

As soon as you begin to wheel the carriage
the baby inside stops crying
as if any where else
has got to be better than here.

Usually his eyes open wide in anticipation,
but very soon he falls fast asleep
from the monotony
of that hope.

Me

I tried to blow up pigeons with bicarbonate
potions.
I built infernos in dense forests of fern
civilisations,
rafted pollution on polystyrene blocks,
fought in streets run by big brothers,
I stole from the church and
scrawled abuse on their walls,
made ramps to fly high
smoked joints to fly higher,
tasted girls under bridges,
threw false parties
faked I.D,
drank dreams under lamp-posts,
ran from the police,
forgot the time all the time
inside a youthful peace.
And you were all there.
We were all there.

How To Build A Father

Begin with a boy.
Make him do a number of things with catapults, insects in jars.
Give him a pet or the freedom to run along the paths of the forest.

Next make him a man.
This mainly means increase his size. Let him forget catapults.
Ensure he has his first loss - that dog or his first love.
Invent something like a wife. Concern him with the daily bread,
choose him a newspaper for reading on the train.

Surprise him with the news.
Later, lay an infant in his arms. Let him look at the face, fear
for the fragile bones that make the skull.
Other than this equip him with very little.

If you fancy it allow him to imagine his significance.
A regular seat by the hearth, custody of the remote control,
now and then, some idea that what he says is true -
will be abided by. Let him also think you're taking his advice
(his half of conversation) don't imagine he's listening.

Lastly make him old.
This mainly means reduce his size. Let him forget
the ends of sentences, look past you with his milky eyes.
(He'll be recalling catapults and forest paths).

In the end just let him go.
Carry his coffin

- if you can shoulder it.

What I Would Tell You

Sometimes

i look at the pictures
of the younger me
and want to reach out
and shake you
and try to stop
you from leading the life
that you did

i would tell you
not to take that job
that ended up making you
ill

i would tell you not
to go to the bar
where you met her
and entered that world
of pain

i would tell you to listen more
and speak less
because your words
got you into so much trouble

i would tell you that
drinking pernod and black
was not the greatest decision
you ever made

and that the snakebite
was something you
should steer clear of

that you should have gone
to america when you
had the chance
and things might
have worked out over
there

but they might not have

and you would have listened
to me and i would have been
wrong

there are people you
should have hated
but loved instead

and people you ignored
who loved you and
would have helped you through
the bad times
when you were alone

but there are things
that i am glad that you did
they made me the man
that you became

and i am grateful for
all the stupid decisions that
you made
because some of
them were the best mistakes
ever

i wonder what the older
me will think
about decisions i am about to
make

this is a long game
and whatever i do
will have consequences

for you

It Goes On

The pain was unreal,
And I knew,
Gut feeling that it was not right.
Dehydration,
That's what they told me,
I would be able to go home tomorrow.
It's fine,
Then life became blurred,
Lost the meaning of hours and days.
I only noticed the pain,
And the tubes and the pain,
And the machines and the pain,
And the beeps and the pain,
And the strangers and the pain,
I heard voices.
What, what?
What was wrong with me?
But no one would tell me.
Drifting between reality and dream.
Between life and death.
I awoke, and the pain was gone.
The person I was died,
Yet I live on.
And I'm making the most of it

Bloaks Of A Surtan Aje

are mizrabul old gits hooo like wimmin
thay can be teenajers wiv
sumwun hooo needs them
choosdys & sundys
fones on mundys & wensdys
thay can ferget on thers & frys
& scroo on saterdys
wen thay will wurry abowt there verillitty

doant relie on them
thay get frytend & run up the rode
as farst as thay can
doant nead them
thay thinck yooo wont there penshun
doant let them no yooo no
its all boolshit
then there wilys woant werk.

they tork alot about there kidz
but yors r thretning
thay state there ayms
for the relayshunship
but piss oaver yors
yooo ners them throo illniss
thay leev yooo in goodniss
thay mayk indisysiv staytmence
of flimzy meening
to no aparant perpus

A Lost Man

i don't know what
to say
when I dial his
number so
i always put the
phone down

he's no longer
there anyway
not the man
he was

i relive good times
a giant of a man
who could inspire
empty rooms

i see only his
shadow now
as he plots his
own downfall

he hides his
pain from us making
cameo appearances in
our lives

dredging up a strength to
fight his demons one more
time

we feel the sap leaving
him and feel helpless
to help him resist

he's becoming a fading
memory
flowing slowly downstream

just out of our reach.

Level II

If life were a video game,
I'd have zapped all the baddies
Wasted all the nasty aliens
And made off to the spaceship with all the loot.

But like all good gamers
I know it doesn't end here.
The words 'Level II - The Terrors of Middle Age'
Ascend to the middle
Of the screen.

And all the equipment that I had accumulated
In my confident destruction of the horrors of the
Previous level are ineffective here.

So, I'm standing here with my obsolete blasters
While the ogres & pitfalls of a solitary middle age
Eagerly close in.

The Man Who Speaks Four Languages

His voice is quiet, his accent's east-European.
He can't afford my grandfather's fees.
They talk in the waiting room, I listen
through a crack in the door. He waves
me in, finds a turquoise behind my ear,
a tourmaline in my dress pocket,
and rattles them together like dice
until they disappear. The next time
I see him, he's carrying a statue.
It's a boy, bending to pull a thorn
from his foot. The man tells me
how it reminds him of running
in woods without shoes, of his mother's
warnings. Now it pays for his teeth.
With it, he hands over too,
all those escape routes he planned,
nights with a knife under his mattress
calculating the depth of a fall, nights
wondering which furniture he could push
against a door, how much time he'd have
to grab the kids, whether he was strong
enough to carry them both, and how far?

Wings

"Waking then was like dreaming.
Waking then was like a lonely dream..."
                    - Yevgeny Yevtushenko

"Waking then was like dreaming," yes.
And dreaming then was like new life,
Like uncurling, and stretching out your limbs
For something unknown and desirable.
Feeling at ease with yourself,
Unshackled.
Like leaning from a window carelessly,
To feel the wind's caress
Of face, and hair:
Drawing breath, and glad to exist.
Glad to be living on these wings.
And every morning, the dawn rising, early.

(The Last Day of Being) Twenty-Six

Today is
The Last Day Of Being Twenty-Six
Middle age and boredom beckon
The fun of pot-bellies and wrinkles
Approach at feverish pace
Extracting the good looks from body
And face.
Cheeky glances from eighteen-year-olds
To be replaced by fat, in folds
The fun of late-night partying
And childish antics
Are overcome by
Life's semantics.

7: WHILE THE SUN DANCED

Feel The Sun

Can you sense it?
Like some benevolent thing
Waiting to welcome you
A little way down the road

Can you smell it?
Like some ephemeral fragrance
A way off across the meadows
That fans the finer emotions within.

Everyone hears its tune
And dances
Crazy hares doing their freestyle
Bop, digging the vibe.

Daffodils choreograph their slo-mo
Rise and explode into colour
At the climax of the piece

Snowdrops and bluebells
Paint their pixelated dreams
For those free to run through
The forest and see.

And in the city
Modern man
So cool, so funky
So removed
Feels it too
And expresses it with a smile
On the way to work
Or especially vybin' off the tunes
Direct-injected in their ears.

We all feel it
As one
Tilt your head skywards
Like the flowers
And feel the sun.

For it begins -
The coming of Spring

Leeds

(day one at the Leeds Festival 2002)

Fast building anticipation.
Around a small wooden table,
In the back room of a pub.
Sat with a motley regiment
Of unrefined camping types
Drinking beer and preparing
For a weekend with a difference.

Braced for the evening chill,
We step outside and seek our steed
A trusty German van built to last
But built too long ago for my liking.
We cram aboard two by two.
And our carriage cries once with the turn of a key
Purring with aged content by the roadside.

We set sail on seas of tarmac and let the devil catch the distance,
The roar of an air cooled engine and the faded dashboard lights
Offer us newfound companionship.
Somewhere in the back,

I hear the crisp clean hiss of opening tins.
I spy my compatriots front and back
Streetlights reflected in their eyes.
As the solemn road begins to move beneath us
Wedged amidst tarpaulin and supplies for self-preservation.
This is our sacred voyage to a not so distant land.

We sail along congested motorways
Part of an ever growing fleet.
Hurried fingers guide us like the stars
As they point to the sterile glow
Of a motorway service station.
We disembark, we represent
The spearhead of an invading conquest
Seeking crisps, and pop and cigarettes.

An American motorhome
Sidles up alongside us.
Its dubious owners
Spy our chariot and smile with contempt.
We are not flash
We are not new
We are worn and frayed at the edges.
And the weekend hasn't even started yet.

The road runs out as quickly as it began.
Greeted by fairground lights
And low clouds in the sky above.
Yellow-jacketed security guides us
Down and round muddy paths
Across fields and through hedges
Our trusty steed pitches and leans
In turmoil against the storm drenched soil

We drop anchor.
In the corner of a field.
Spared by the shade of some bushes
We land first and stake our claim.
This field will be our weekend nation.

Now the first battle commences.

The tent lunges out of the darkness to fight with me.
I wrestle with its bone pegs and its mottled tarpaulin flesh
It unravels around me, trying to snag my arms and legs.
We engage our enemy by force and stretch its dayglo skin
Make it fit the arched and buckled bones.
Our opponent becomes our home.

This is our first night.

Sleep is not an option.

We cram from our tent and I claim the passenger seat of the van
The rain peters out and I see the stars through the condensation streaks on glass.
Idle banter ensues and the engine is started for our perpetual warmth.
Never mind the poor sods nearby
At risk from ground level exhaust.

Friday morning when I'm usually at work
Instead I bear the scars of the outdoor life.
I fell asleep on grass
Only to wake bearing nature's print across my face.

Half staggered itineraries are planned.
Over hurried ramshackle breakfasts
And it all tastes nice if you don't let it linger
In the mouth or on the tongue.

We go out on foot.
A half hour trek to the stages
Where we will spend our days.
Heavy footfalls on mud and grass
And plastic sheetings
An assembled march before the music starts.

83

We approach the wide angled fences
And we are herded through like cattle.
Police dogs and handlers look us up and down.
Like statistics and numbers.
I'm frisked and asked if I'm carrying.
I give my answer and kneel to pat the dog.
Beer for breakfast has given me a sunny disposition.

Those first few hours under clear skies
And I feel the lively tingle of sunburn beginning.
Red faced but relaxed atop a grassy mound
While the best local comedy has to offer
Offers itself upon a plate to us
Brave souls these that would tickle
A sleep deprived crowd on the first day
Still reliving tent-related nightmares.

Food stalls offer exotic fare
That looks surprisingly free
Of microbes and fungi
That would leave me doubled
With weekend cramps
And poisoned sweats and shakes.
I chance a meat-free option
And live to write these words.

We try to lay down plans of where we'll be and what we'll see.
Points of contact should the need arise
If we split and separate and lose ourselves in crowds
To be lost in a sea of joyous limbs
Washed away on tides of sound

Nonentity bands litter the bill like flotsam and jetsam
And we drift from one to another armed with lukewarm beer in bendy plastic cups
Already crunching underfoot from the careless carefree revellers.
Nothing holds our interest and our unsettled legion begins to disperse
I touch base and make camp by a van selling tea.
The woman behind the counter has a friendly face
So I trust her with my change and the safety of my health.

Peaches

I'm in the cramped confines of the Carling tent
Bumper to bumper with bodies
Some have already forsaken the natural act of standing
And everybody seems to be leaning one way or the other.
Everybody supporting everybody else.
The stage is consumed with speakers of impossible size
And mythical capacity.
I'm unsure what to expect

I know of the act and I've heard some of their songs.
But the visual will only remain a mystery for a moment longer.

It's like being somewhere tacky.
The crowd entertained with this mock seventies New York performance.
Lewd and crude with bad sound and gyrating dancing
Songs about fucking delivered with menace.
I'm too near the front for my liking
And the woman in front is leaning back so far I think she's trying to pass through me.

Peaches stares at my friend and his inner self shrieks with fear
She could pounce from the stage and tear him to pieces
Her eyes linger and I daren't laugh
I would never give her the ammunition
To turn her attack upon me.
Forty minutes pass in amusement and tension.

After she's gone it's like being able to breathe again.
The crush subsides and the moist heat of the crowd relinquishes slowly
The ground has become a plastic ocean punctured by patches of flattened grass.
Nature sustains casualties in our name and I wonder just how many blades fell
so we could enjoy and endure in equal measures our distinctive decibel pleasures.

The sun begins to slide from the sky
And shadows all around us lengthen.

As we move from one place to another.
I use the time filled with mediocre bands
To seek hot tea from the trusted stall which will become my second home.

Trudging up and down steep inclines
Leg tendons lengthen and knees deepen
And I feel like a spider trying to climb the sides of a bath.
An absence of flat ground distorts the view and the muscles
And people drop where they can with beers in hand
While I find my stride and drag past the commercial tents

Wherever you walk there is sound to be embraced
Carried on the breeze it ebbs and flows tempting you forward
To follow its ethereal trail and surrender to its charms.
More songs are playing and crucial decisions need to be made.
The telephone text message has never been more important than now.

Abbreviated messages wink back and forth between handsets
In the blink of an eye our scattered forces begin to reunite.
Dragged from the four corners of this miniature Earth
This glass bubble existence has made me forget home, forget everything.

Prodigy

Three quarters back

It's almost dark. The air scented with charcoal.
I watch a fire juggler
His flash bronze fire sticks flare
casting butterfly shadows on the ground.

Beside me
someone from home
is on the pull
Sidling closer to a dreadlocked girl with promises of warm beer
And a read of his festival programme. She nods and smiles dumbly
With satellite dish eyes she is only receiving on one frequency.
Agenda foiled, said individual gives up gracefully and remembers why he is here.

The stage in darkness like an open mouth.
the glint of metal flashing off a drum kit
And neon corporate logos
spiral up and down the vast acreage of screens
That aid our pinprick view of the stage.
Slowly sound filters in low and dark swooping across the fields.
and the static of conversation dries away to nothing.

A simple bass line.
Dark and guttural claiming all it finds.
A slow burning fuse has been lit, crowd transfixed
Cheers rise from the front rolling like water over the crowd

And one by one people around me are uprooted from the ground
Brought to their feet in mesmerised pleasure.

Suddenly it begins
Flashbulb white lights rip through the night and bathe the crowd in sparks of ivory.
Percussion falls in waves like hammers and the senses register full
Hackles rise as adrenaline surges through this collective
People move shout bounce dance scream.
A bomb burst of sound has just detonated
And nowhere on Earth can feel like this right now.

Singers and Rappers stalk the stage
Enigmatic cinematic presences spitting words
With mock rage and incandescent delivery.
Sweat-driven fury as voice and instrument
Collide in the air as one sneering sound replaces the last.

We stand like zombies
Submissive to the performance
Our energy drained like blood from our bodies.
Gripped in vices of emotion as the raw delivery
Takes us places we seldom visit.

The Streets

I forsake the hung drawn and quartered vocals of Guns and Roses
For more sedate climes and begin my emergency rendezvous with the dance tent.
Moving in complete darkness I unfold out through the maze of people.
Quick agitated paths are planned and I seek shortcuts through the maze of tents.
Feet drag on cobweb rope lines and I stumble fold and fall on the soft ground.
Knees first unhurt I recover limbs and composure and upright balance.
I'm following others who run on ahead like straight lined soldiers.

The tent is all sides open and each gap spills people like a wound.
Their full frontal stares as they wait and I see steam rising from cramped and clenched bodies
I'm too far from the stage but the soundcheck opens and I catch every note.

This will have to do.

It's a worthy cause I've fought for
Catching a band in their infancy
Venue small relatively
Crowd passionate definitely
Audience pleasers assuredly
Taking the stage confidently.

I see a laid back stoner's set.
The beats never rise too far too fast or too high

And songs that are becoming rapidly familiar
Play upon my training ear.
I take my slice of urban poetry with more than just a pinch of salt
There's truth in those words and I relate to the horizontal Nintendo tales.
The British contingent that doesn't spout guns or crack or smack
Just moderation stories of a herbal extraction.

Deep breathing everybody…and relax.

End of Part One…

Curfew enforced let fresh battle be joined
As people stream back to their tents like tears.
Feet slide along grass and the rivers they forge become oceans
Pace slows as woodland habitat beckons.
Conversation comes in all shapes and sizes
And we trudge head down on dust-dry soil.
Cutting a swathe right down the middle
Of a fading day one war zone.
Jokes and shouts are fired from one side to another
I'm walking on no man's land.
Distant radios shape the air with angst-filled teenage music
The night is bathed in the smell of teen spirit.

Field

Mummy in the Volvo estate
waits in the field for
Georgina and friends

Mummy with the stern auburn perm,
good strong hands
and corduroy legs

Farmer's wife in fleece, Tory stalwart

Georgina with the pigtails and hair braid
peachy skin and cut offs
voice hoarse all yelled out

For three cheap beer nights
in the orange and blue one man tent
Georgina took a ride

With the eager hips of

Darren all the way from Leeds
dreadlocks and combats
dirty fingernails, Moroccan breath

Georgina dips her head
Mummy holds her tight
Darren fucks off

Taking his golden cherry.

Open House

The door opens onto the crowded vista
of her frame, Tuleka's sound escapes her lips: "Awe".
In the corner the chunky red bike leans precariously
delirious from its French country escape to a London yuppie setting,
its seat serves as holder to the phone, translucent gimmicky technology
it rings sporadically of its own accord, adding crazy conversation to the smell
of boiling rice, the scent of washing machine detergent-washed clothes, and the
chatter-chatter of the blue box; Amira zonked from work, watching it in spectacular
baby faced adore, with eyes that light up on my arrival, head tilted to the left, eyes
smiling, body reluctant to give up the space that is the red cloaked sofa-bed that's seen
many a guest, sleeping and riding their dreams into the dead end of slumber and
waking up on the reality train that is sometimes cornflakes and weird vanilla milk and
maybe

pancakes or some sort of omelette waiting in the hands of those reluctantly awake 'cos
there is lectures, or a long day of dossing before essays must be done, in this tower
block are some of those whom I hold dear way up high, in this experiment where
music is made for love and considered, like the thought of making babies and
growing old together and laughing while we ride the blowback of love from friend to
friend to friend to friend to friend to friend.

Infinite Blue Sky

I remember the dawn
Seeping through the gaps
In the curtains
And I, with an ascending
Hope
Dancing around my sternum
Would pull the curtain back
To find out whether we
Were to be bathed in sunshine
Or to be oppressed by the
Nondescript grey
Of an all-too-familiar
English summers day.

But each dawn surprised
And caressed me with the
Warmth
Love
And beauty of another
Infinite blue sky.
And while the sun danced
In the east (over Eastbourne)
My heart would fill with
The joy of the presence
Of good friends and sunshine.

And soon we would rise
And sleepily converse, make
Breakfast and head off
To our summer jobs
Making plans for the
Evenings,
Preparing ourselves to love.

I would sometimes
Cycle or sometimes
Hitch-hike to the university
Assaulted by the scents
Of the flora lining the
Roads
Astounded by the parched
Dry fields, my imagination
Raced; this summer England

Looks mediterranean - this
Could be Provence. This
Could be Spain.

And at work we'd be lazy
And slow. We'd pass the
Time and take long lunchbreaks
Sitting on the grass (or
Sometimes supping pints in
The pub) laughing and sharing
Love. It's like the sunshine
Gave us the key to the
Ability to love.

And in the evenings we'd
Drink. Sit in a beer
Garden somewhere, telling
Tales and laughing
And walking home beneath
A sultry sulky moon
Until we'd collapse in bed
And make love and then
Fall asleep with
Honeysuckle-inspired dreams
Forming in the unconscious
Part of our minds.

And then the dawn again
Seeping through the gaps
In the curtains.
I'd pull the curtains back
And be caressed by the warmth
Love and beauty of another
Infinite blue sky...

Party

The room's filling up with people I've known.
They leave wine circles on the mantelpiece,
open windows, change tapes in the cassette,
flick through books and photo albums.
Someone's taken yesterday's paper from the bin
and is looking for a story. They tell each other
about themselves, kiss at the bottom of the stairs,
turn down lights and move into the garden with cushions
and rugs. They eat bite-sized tarts and tread on toys,
twist hair and press pendants into thumbs, scratch and cough.
Some have come back from the dead. They cling to drainpipes
and stand on shoulders, stretch for upstairs windows.
The hall is packed and cars fill the road, spill up side streets - they've
reached the racecourse. Floorboards give way,
collapse into the cellar. The music's so loud it interrupts
my heartbeat. My clothes are handed out to those who are cold.
All the paper in the house is torn up to write numbers on.
They take over the cemetery. A hotel pianist
and bass-player I fancied set up a stage with fallen
headstones. Friends with children organise a crèche.
A succession of plumbers who never understood my boiler
spot-weld standpipes. The detectives and para from Aldershot
who once lived upstairs, arrange a military display.
Part-time djs - van driver, computer salesman
and personal trainer from the gym - spin three decades,
45s to CDs. All the men I've ever been out with
are put in discussion groups by women friends.
Women from the ferries, shops, kennels, bars, temp agencies
and language school arrange shift work at minimal pay
for the handful of chief executives who've shown up. Relatives
have comfortable chairs away from the party
and all those cash-only landlords offer free rooms overnight.
Photographers take polaroids of everyone.
A man from the allotments hands out runner bean poles
and the electricians run a cable to a photocopier.
Every face is enlarged to the size of a flag
as in demonstrations for the missing - husbands, wives,
toddlers, teenagers, street children, grandfathers,
aunts, cousins, neighbours, workmates, friends.

Deux Mille Trois

And just when I thought she'd gone
That she'd vanished abruptly in the night
Without giving me a chance to hug her
And say a tearful adieu

She returns, turns up
Unannounced
At my door
As if resurrected
Streaming beautiful light into the
Heart of me.

And let me hold you
You, like no other. Let me caress
Your sunlight face for the last time
Let me walk with you down green
Silent valleys, with llamas and
Blue skies our companions

Let us lay and be still and take the
Time to soak up each others' company
For I do not know when I will see
You or one like you again.

You gave me the most beautiful times
And memories that will reverberate in me
I promise
Until the very day I die.

Adieu l'été deux mille trois
For you were truly blessed.

Bubbles

This happiness
Watching a thousand bubbles drifting across a deep blue sky
Each one producing a perfect pearlescent rainbow as it catches the light
A thousand bubbles producing smiles on the sun-scorched faces of those below them.
Trapping a thousand memories of a perfect snapshot of this perfect happiness

8: HE THOUGHT IT WAS REAL

Every Other Me

I am not your resolution, I am the contraflow
I am your subconscious fantasy
I am the wild goose chase down a blind alley
I am the hole in the road by the broken street light
I do not have the blueprint
I do not have the master key
I don't have to give you answers
I have nothing up my sleeve
I am the slow puncture
I am every wrong lottery number
I am the buffers at the end of the line
I am every hidden trapdoor
I want to be everything you're not
I am the B side, the afterthought
I am the shiny happy hippy chick
I am the speck in the distance
I am the one you can't put down to experience
I am the rock, and the soft place to fall
I am atomic, I am supersonic
I am not your four leaf clover, but I am your supernova

Our Last Supper Together in a Cemetery

My love, I know you have a penchant for the recherché.
But why did you insist we dine
In this restaurant among skeletons.
The opening on the front of your black pants suit
That revealed your scanty black brassiere
And the freckled flesh of the sides of your breasts
Persuaded me.

I noted everyone drinks white wine and has no eyes.
I recognized we were dining in a cemetery.
You did all the talking, you always do.
You talked about BMW's, bank vaults,
The stock market, how you, naked,
Like to ride tap-dancing horses over old battlefields.
You opened your portfolio,
Spread before me; formulas, blue-prints,
Plans for bank robberies,
And a piece of white stained glass
That was once part of a lamb
On a stained-glass window.
I said to her, "This is a strange place
For lovers to dine."
She replied, "This is the only place
Lovers dine in our postmodern times."
As the sky dims, glass candles were turned on.
Wax fireflies flew over our heads and glowed.
She said, "When the shadow
Of the wax firefly crosses my lips,
You can kiss me."

Kicking Small Dogs

A confession: each small dog I see
I want to kick.

Usually I am ambivalent,
in a canine sense,

but small dogs, shoebox size,
move me.

It is not cruelty, or an urge to inflict pain,
but natural curiosity.

A long run:
arc of bootswing

meeting small dog
and soft underbelly.

I need to know how far they would fly;
it is a science:

are the houses over the road in range?
Open windows, buses, rugby posts

all cry out to be used:
apparatus of discovery.

In my dreams the dogs are silent;
the sky is always blue, cloudless,
and it is perfect.

It's About Time

Remember
It is necessary to be here
As you read this to yourself
Notice
How lonely this place is now
Peaceful as any old cemetery
Here and now
is a place we rarely ever visit
Isn't it?
Remember
It is necessary to remember
What is going to happen here
Notice
How different things can seem
if we slipslide into a daydream
Paying attention
Would come easy then, wouldn't it?

Zebra

He thought it was real,
and it filled him with paranoia
he tried to run away,
but there was nowhere to go
he shouted at it to go away,
and for me to stop it messing with his head.
he began to shake,
and I could tell he was going to lose it,
He was dripping sweat,
and his eyes started rolling in his head.
Then I had to explain that it was only a man dressed as a zebra

Questions About Loss *For Erich Fried*

Which would you rather lose:
Your religion,
Your lover,
Or your mind? *Choose.*
What reason do you have for this?

Did you lose one once,
Or come close to it?
Was it mislaid, or neglected?
Or did you wave goodbye
Still smiling?

When did you find it was gone?
Too late?

And, did you find another?
Soon, or a long time afterwards?
Was it the same as the one you lost?
Did you like it as much?

Would you rather go back
To the beginning
And start again?

Leaking Kerosene

leaking kerosene
jettison the excess, trailing vapours
let it all fall away
this miscalculation
running on empty, nothing left to give
misjudged, misread so badly
falling out of the sky, leaking kerosene
how fast the ground comes up

Eyes In Midnight Skies

Like a two-way stream of moonbeam catching
eyes in midnight skies, my soul cruises a time of
night that leaves daylight paralysed.

Again night asks me,
'What have you learnt?'

I saw mushroom clouds
silence loud
people drown
inside a frown.
Neglected children's
brains rotting
animals take their turn
to burn
mild mothers die
in front of child
run by oak masters
grown truly wild.
I saw new-born embryos
scream
fantastic dreams
to be
dropped
inside an intuitive sphere.

What have I learnt from you?

To cry with open eyes
that live inside all lives.
For I am but a cosmic pet,
mentally muzzled
by an absent vet
who returns
to see what has been learnt.
Your dark Intelligence deals in catatonic
apocalyptic peoples that
pursue perceptions of pre-conceived destiny.
Ill-fated testimony.
Futures are delegated that
would explode souls,
we disbelieve?
Once warned we mocked

Like Neverlands high on false eternity
block locked
our minds mourned
but I dance beneath in what you made
for me to wade.
In days of night my muzzle releases
a million worlds of alien belief
that spasm my mind in disbelief
as I skip around your Intelligence.

What have I learnt?

I learnt you.

Living random
in tandem with
you
I move in time
no love from no sun
I became you
became I
became we
became one.

The Poets

Section 1: BEHIND MY DESK

Monday Morning	Sundra
Rodent Olympics	New City Scribe
Nine To Five	Judith Brown
Computer Solitaire	Karen Alkalay-Gut
I Tell Her How Much I Despise Work	Brad Evans
Trash Girl	Linda Rosenkrans
Deepest Afternoon	New City Scribe
Resistance Is Futile	Brad Evans

Section 2: EVERYONE IS TRAVELLING

Afghan Market, Peshawar	Victoria Field
Praha	Liana Hemmett
In A Lonely Crowd - Near Nagoya Station	Christopher Andrews
Not In Africa	Matt Gambrill
Zao mi je	Liana Hemmett
River	Duane Locke
The Sadness Of Stations	Matt Gambrill
Letters Home	Susan Richardson
Platform	Alison Dunne
No Point To Being A Slow Lemming	Subash Raman
Baggage Claim	Susan Richardson

Section 3: A NIGHT LIKE THIS

Dinner With A Tyrant	Judith Brown
The Girl In The Nightclub	Brad Evans
Milk	Adrian Carter
Too Much	Josephine Burns
Singing At Stars	Martin Burke
Waiting	Sarah Fordham
A Charm Against Insomnia	Karen Alkalay-Gut

Section 4: SOME QUIET CONVERSATION

Edible Poems	Karen Alkalay-Gut
To The Desperate And The Proud	Brad Evans
Polemical/Poetical	Sarah Annetts
Communication	Adrian Carter
Reaching Out	Sarah Annetts

Section 5: THE WEIGHT OF LOVE

You	Anthea Campbell
Silvered	Alison Dunne
The Furthest Edge	Jenny Freeman
Heavenly Body	Liana Hemmett

Synchronicity	Sarah Annetts
Lucky For Some	Susan Richardson
A Surfer	Mandy Tsang
Absence	Dele Fatunla
Breaking Up	Judith Brown
Red Gold and Green	New City Scribe
November	Sarah Annetts
The Touch	Jenny Freeman
Loneliness	Alessandro Mascia
Ciao Bella	New City Scribe

Section 6: THE TIME ALL THE TIME

Minding The Infant	Karen Alkalay-Gut
Me	David McCullough
How To Build A Father	Alison Dunne
What I Would Tell You	Martin Togher
It Goes On	Josephine Burns
Bloaks Of A Surtan Aje	Jenny Freeman
Level II	New City Scribe
A Lost Man	Martin Togher
The Man Who Speaks Four Languages	Jackie Wills
Wings	Sarah Annetts
(The Last Day of Being) Twenty-Six	New City Scribe

Section 7: WHILE THE SUN DANCED

Feel The Sun	New City Scribe
Leeds	Adrian Carter
Field	Liana Hemmett
Open House	Dele Fatunla
Infinite Blue Sky	New City Scribe
Party	Jackie Wills
Deux Mil Trois	New City Scribe
Bubbles	Josephine Burns

Section 8: HE THOUGHT IT WAS REAL

Every Other Me	Nessy
Our Last Supper Together in a Cemetery	Duane Locke
Kicking Small Dogs	Matt Gambrill
It's About Time	Subash Raman
Zebra	Josephine Burns
Questions About Loss	Sarah Annetts
Leaking Kerosene	Nessy
Eyes In Midnight Skies	David McCullough

The Editors

Sarah Annetts grew up in Birmingham, became addicted to poetry as a teenager, and has made no effort to quit the habit since.

The discovery of vibrant modern poetry - "words that burn" as Thomas Gray said - and international voices - was a revelation after a rather stodgy diet of Shakespeare, Keats and Tennyson at school. She started to write seriously, inspired by poetic heroes as diverse as Raymond Carver, Erich Fried and Bono.

Sarah studied at Bristol University and now works as a GP, which allows her the great privilege of dealing with people from all walks of life. She is co-editor of the Scriberazone, having been a contributing poet from the site's early days.

Peter Johnson was born in London in 1964. He grew up as part of the West Indian community in the north-west of the city. Music led to him becoming seriously interested in poetry when he heard Linton Kwesi Johnson's *Dread Beat and Blood* featured on a BBC2 documentary. In subsequent years he attempted to write dub poetry, and was featured at age seventeen in UK publication *Caribbean Times*. His poetic instincts subsequently found a performance outlet through rap and reggae spoken forms, all the while writing formal poetry in private.

He left London in 1987 and lived in Buckinghamshire, Oxford, and Brighton in turn. This period resulted in a shift in his approach to art and life. He founded *Inspire*, a what's on magazine in Oxford and then studied Social Psychology at Sussex University.

In 1998 he returned to London where he founded Scriberazone, and began holding live events which featured poetry, live music and DJs. He views these *Words & Beats*, *Literary Lounge* and *NuPoetics* events as the natural synthesis of the varied cultural, artistic and poetic influences that he has been exposed to over the years.

Peter now lives in Sheffield, South Yorkshire.

Acknowledgements

Scriberazone would like to thank all the poets, writers, artists and other creatives who have sent work to us or contributed to the things we do. We're always amazed at how much talent you people out there have and it's great that you choose to share it with us.

Also a big thank you to those who have helped us in our endeavours over the years; including, but certainly not limited to, Andrea Burns, Emma Midgley, Jennifer Nikkel, Jessica York, Jo Burns, Karen Alkalay-Gut, Martin Togher, Paul Annetts, Rachel Norman, Rick Goodale, Sam Jones, Sarah Fordham, and Verity Sharp (for airing one of our poetry/music creations on national radio).

Finally to the audiences. We creatives exist on attention, therefore all this would be meaningless without you! So we dedicate this book to the attendees at our Words & Beats, Literary Lounge and NuPoetics events, to those of you who listened to us perform at the Big Chill festival in 2003 and 2004, and of course to the many thousands of visitors to our website over the years.

In addition, the editors and publishers would like to thank the following for their permission to use copyright material:

Adrian Carter for 'Milk', 'Communication', 'Leeds'; Alison Dunne for 'Platform', 'Silvered', 'How To Build A Father'; Anthea Campbell for 'You'; Brad Evans for 'I Tell Her How Much I Despise Work', 'Resistance Is Futile', 'The Girl In The Nightclub', 'To The Desperate And The Proud'; Christopher Andrews for 'In A Lonely Crowd - Near Nagoya Station'; David McCullough for 'Me', 'Eyes In Midnight Skies'; Dele Fatunla for 'Absence', 'Open House'; Duane Locke for 'River', 'Our Last Supper Together In A Cemetery'; Jackie Wills for 'The Man Who Speaks Four Languages' and 'Party' from *Party* (Leviathan, 2004); Jenny Freeman for 'The Furthest Edge', 'The Touch', 'Bloaks Of A Surtan Aje'; Josephine Burns for 'Too Much', 'It Goes On', 'Bubbles', 'Zebra'; Judith Brown for 'Nine To Five', 'Dinner With A Tyrant', 'Breaking Up'; Karen Alkalay-Gut for 'Computer Solitaire', 'A Charm Against Insomnia', 'Edible Poems', 'Minding The Infant'; Liana Hemmett for 'Praha' and 'Zao mi je' from *On The Edge* (Koo Press, 2005), 'Heavenly Body', 'Field'; Linda Rosenkrans for 'Trash Girl'; Martin Burke for 'Singing At Stars'; Martin Togher for 'What I Would Tell You', 'A Lost Man'; Matt Gambrill for 'Not In Africa', 'The Sadness Of Stations', 'Kicking Small Dogs'; Nessy for 'Every Other Me', 'Leaking Kerosene'; Sarah Fordham for 'Waiting'; Sundra for 'Monday Morning' from *Starchild* (2003); Susan Richardson for 'Letters Home', 'Baggage Claim', 'Lucky For Some'; Victoria Field for 'Afghan Market, Peshawar' from *Olga's Dreams* (Fal Publications, 2004); Iowa University International Writing Program (IWP) for the extract used on page 45, taken from *Selected Poems* by Agnes Nemes Nagy (trans. B. Berlind, IWP 1980).

The publishers have made every effort to trace copyright holders, but in some cases without success. We shall be glad to hear from anyone who has been inadvertently overlooked or incorrectly cited and will make the necessary changes at the first opportunity.

Find out more about *Scriberazone* and our poets, as well as our multimedia poetry & music mixes by visiting our website:

http://www.scriberazone.co.uk

We encourage poets, writers & artists to share their work with us.

Email: submissions@scriberazone.co.uk